EASY MICROWAVE HOMEMADE TREATS

NATIONAL
LIBRARY
OF AUSTRALIA

A catalogue record for this book is available from the National Library of Australia

Published 2021

ISBN: 978-0-6453437-8-6 (ebook)
ISBN: 978-0-6453437-9-3 (paperback)

9 780645 343793

Published by Jumble Books and Publishers
(https://jumblebooksandpublishers.com)

IMAGE CREDIT

"Baking Day" by William Hemsley (1817 or 1819-1906), 1893.
Image is in the public domain.

Easy Microwave Homemade Treats

Fudges, brittles, etc

Julie Morrigan

CONTENTS

THINGS TO NOTE WHEN COOKING TREATS

Although these treats are generally quick and easy to make, working with hot liquid sugar and chocolate may be dangerous so please be careful and take note of the following:

- Remember that these treats will be very hot when cooking and take all safety precautions necessary.

- It is important to use a non-plastic microwave-safe bowl or jug during the cooking process. Plain glass bowls or jugs are not recommended as they may shatter at the temperatures involved. Borosilicate cookware (such as Pyrex) is generally safe to use in making fudges, brittles or toffees.

- If using cling film (or plastic wrap), do not let it come into contact with the contents of the bowl or the jug during the cooking process as it will melt.

- Baking paper can be used over foil or in place of greasing baking trays. Only use oven-safe baking dishes and trays.

- Remember to soak any dishes used for cooking in hot water as soon as they have been emptied. This will make it easier to clean them in the normal way later. Make sure the water is hot (not boiling) before it comes into contact with the jugs or bowls as suddenly coming into contact with cold water while still being hot may cause the jugs or bowls to shatter.

- Chocolate holds its shape when melted in a microwave so will need to be stirred with a dry metal spoon.

- Children making any of these treats should be closely supervised.

- Waiting until the treats are cold before eating them is difficult but strongly recommended.

- Have fun!

WHITE CHRISTMAS

Ingredients
1 cup powdered milk
1 cup coconut
1 cup icing sugar
1 cup mixed fruit
½ cup chopped nuts
1½ cups rice bubbles
Vanilla
240 g copha

Method
1. Mix all dry ingredients and vanilla.
2. Melt copha, add to dry ingredients, mix well.
3. Form into balls or press in flat tin, then cut into squares when firm.
4. Keep in cool place.

ROCKY ROAD

Ingredients
85 g (1 cup) desiccated coconut
115 g (1 cup) walnut pieces, roughly chopped
400 g dark chocolate melts
30 g copha, finely chopped
250 g marshmallows

Method
1. Line base and sides of a 16.5 x 26 cm lamington pan with baking paper.
2. Place the coconut in an oven bag and twist the bag to close. Place on the microwave turntable and cook on HIGH (100%), shaking the bag every minute, for 2-4 minutes or until the coconut is lightly toasted. Remove from microwave and transfer the coconut to a plate to cool.
3. Place the walnuts in an oven bag and twist the bag to close. Cook on HIGH (100%), shaking the bag every minute, for 2-3 minutes or until the walnuts are lightly toasted. Transfer to plate with the coconut.
4. Place chocolate in a microwave-safe bowl. Add the copha pieces. Heat, uncovered, on MEDIUM (50%), stirring every minute with a metal spoon, for 4-5 minutes or until the chocolate and copha melts. Remove from the microwave and stir until smooth.
5. Add the coconut, walnuts and marshmallows and stir until well combined. Spread the mixture into the prepared pan. Place in the fridge for 2 hours or until set. Cut into 24 squares.

SHERRY BALLS

Ingredients
1 packet milk arrowroot biscuits
240 g icing sugar
1 cup mixed fruit
1 tablespoon sherry
Vanilla to taste
1 tablespoon cocoa
240 g butter
Coconut

Method
1. Crush biscuits with rolling pin.
2. Melt butter.
3. Mix all dry ingredients, pour over butter, sherry and vanilla. Mix well.
4. Roll into balls, roll in coconut.

RUM BALLS

Ingredients
4 cups cake or biscuit crumbs
2 tablespoons icing sugar
2 tablespoons cocoa
240 g butter
2 tablespoons condensed milk
2 tablespoons rum
2 drops almond essence
4 drops vanilla

Method
1. Melt butter in saucepan.
2. Stir in cocoa and sugar, heat until both are dissolved.
3. Remove saucepan from heat, stir in rum, essences and condensed milk.
4. Pour mixture over crumbs, mix well.
5. Roll into small balls, toss in chocolate cake topping.

Note—Keep in refrigerator during hot weather.

APRICOT BALLS

Ingredients
240 g dried apricots
½ tin sweetened condensed milk
120 g coconut
60 g chopped nuts

Method
1. Mince apricots. Add coconut, nuts and condensed milk. Mix well.
2. Roll into small balls, coat with icing sugar or coconut.

CHERRY PISTACHIO BARK

Ingredients
250 g white chocolate, broken
155 g toasted chopped pistachios (or walnuts)
65 g dried cherries or dried cranberries (Craisins)

Method
1. Line a baking sheet with foil.
2. Melt chocolate in a microwave-bowl for 1 minute at MEDIUM (50%) for 1 minute and stir until smooth (microwave at medium for 15 seconds additionally if necessary to melt).
3. Stir in most of the nuts and cherries. Spread onto baking sheet, then sprinkle with remaining nuts and cherries.
4. Cool and break into chunks. Keep for up to 1 week in an airtight container.

CARAMELS

Ingredients
1½ cups brown sugar
440 g can condensed milk
125 g butter, chopped
1 tablespoon golden syrup
1 tablespoon liquid glucose

Method
1. Place sugar, condensed milk, butter, syrup and glucose in a large microwave-safe bowl. Mix well.
2. Microwave on HIGH (100%) for 4-5 minutes, stirring once.
3. Cook for a further 8-10 minutes on MEDIUM HIGH (70%), stirring every 2 minutes.
4. Blend in vanilla.
5. Spread mixture into a foil-lined 18 x 28 cm lamington tin.
6. Refrigerate until beginning to set then mark into squares.
7. Chill until set and cut into squares.
8. Store in an airtight container in refrigerator.

GLASS TOFFEE

Ingredients
1 cup white sugar
½ corn syrup or liquid glucose
Food colouring and/or flavouring

Method
1. Mix the sugar and syrup in a large microwave-safe bowl.
2. Cover with cling film and microwave on HIGH (100%) for 2-3 minutes. Do not let it overflow. Do not stir.
3. Cover with new cling film and microwave on HIGH (100%) for another 2-3 minutes.
4. Carefully stir in desired colour and/or flavouring.
5. Quickly pour onto baking paper and allow to harden, shatter, serve.

CASHEW BRITTLE

Ingredients
1½ cups caster sugar
½ cup corn syrup or liquid glucose
1 cup cashews
30 g butter
1½ teaspoons bicarbonate soda
1 teaspoon vanilla essence

Method
1. Combine sugar and corn syrup in a large microwave-safe bowl, stir in cashews.
2. Microwave on HIGH (100%) for 8-10 minutes, stirring twice.
3. Blend in butter, bicarbonate soda and vanilla until foaming.
4. Pour onto a greased baking tray, spreading as thinly as possible.
5. Allow to cool before breaking into pieces.
6. Store in an airtight container.

PEANUT BRITTLE

Ingredients
1½ cups dry roasted peanuts
1 cup white sugar
½ cup light corn syrup or liquid glucose
1 pinch salt (optional)
1 tablespoon butter
1 teaspoon vanilla extract
1 teaspoon bicarbonate soda

Method
1. Grease a baking sheet, and set aside. In a microwave-safe bowl, combine peanuts, sugar, corn syrup, and salt. Cook in microwave for 6-7 minutes on HIGH (100%); mixture should be bubbly and peanuts browned.
2. Stir in butter and vanilla; cook 2-3 minutes longer.
3. Quickly stir in bicarbonate soda, just until mixture is foamy.
4. Pour immediately onto greased baking sheet.
5. Let cool 15 minutes, or until set. Break into pieces, and store in an airtight container.

CHOCOLATE-DIPPED HONEYCOMB

Ingredients
1½ cups (335 g) white sugar
½ cup (125 ml) honey
⅓ cup (80 ml) water
2 tablespoons golden syrup
2 teaspoons bicarbonate soda
200 g baking dark chocolate, chopped

Method
1. Line a baking dish with aluminium foil; grease generously; set aside.
2. Combine sugar, honey, water and golden syrup in a large microwave-safe bowl. Cook on HIGH (100%) for 3 minutes. Stir several times.
3. Continue to cook on HIGH 7-10 minutes, until mixture has thickened (or a small amount separates into hard and brittle threads when dropped in very cold water).
4. Quickly stir in bicarbonate soda, blending completely. The mix will expand considerably.
5. Pour into baking dish, tilting to cover bottom. Let cool until firm, about 1 hour.
6. Break honeycomb into pieces and set aside.
7. Melt dark chocolate in a microwave-safe bowl on HIGH (100%) for 2 minutes. Stir to thoroughly melt. Dip honeycomb pieces into chocolate.
8. Let cool on baking paper. Store in airtight container.

TURKISH DELIGHT

Ingredients
¼ cup powdered gelatine
2 cups caster sugar
¾ cup cornflour
1⅓ cups icing sugar
¼ teaspoon cream of tartar
½ teaspoon rosewater
1 to 2 drops red food colouring
½ cup pistachio kernels, roughly chopped
75 g milk chocolate, chopped

Method
1. Lightly grease a 4 cm deep, 17.5 cm x 27.5 cm slice pan. Line base and sides with baking paper, allowing a 2 cm overhang at both long ends.
2. Place 2½ cups hot water in a large microwave-safe bowl. Sprinkle gelatine over water. Using a fork, whisk until gelatine dissolves. Stir in caster sugar. Microwave, uncovered, on HIGH (100%) for 5 minutes. Stir well. Microwave, uncovered, on HIGH (100%) for a further 4-5 minutes or until mixture is thick and syrupy.
3. Whisk cornflour, icing sugar and cream of tartar into gelatine mixture. Microwave on HIGH (100%) for 3 minutes. Stir in rosewater, food colouring and pistachios. Pour into prepared pan. Refrigerate until firm.
4. Remove Turkish delight from pan. Using a hot knife (see *Note*), cut into 3 cm squares. Remove squares to a new sheet of baking paper.
5. Place chocolate in a microwave-safe bowl. Microwave on HIGH (100%) for 1-2 minutes, stirring with a metal spoon every 30 seconds, or

until melted and smooth. Spoon chocolate into a
snap-lock bag. Snip off 1 corner. Pipe chocolate
over squares. Stand at room temperature until
set. Serve.

Note—To heat knife, hold under hot, running water
for 1 minute or stand in a jug of hot water for 1
minute. Store Turkish delight in an airtight
container in the refrigerator for up to 3 days.

WALNUT FUDGE

Ingredients
3 cups milk chocolate melts
440 g can condensed milk
60 g butter, chopped
1 cup chopped walnuts (or other nuts)

Method
1. Place chocolate, condensed milk and butter in a large microwave-safe bowl.
2. Microwave on MEDIUM (50%) for 4-5 minutes or until chocolate is melted, stir 2 or 3 times during cooking.
3. Blend in walnuts then pour into a foil-lined 18 x 28 cm lamington tin.
4. Refrigerate until firm. Cut into fingers to serve.
5. Store in an airtight container in refrigerator.

MAPLE FUDGE

Ingredients
454 g icing sugar
3 tablespoons milk
1 tablespoon maple syrup
½ cup butter
¾ cup chopped walnuts

Method
1. Line a baking dish with cling film.
2. Sift the icing sugar into a large, microwave-safe bowl. Add the milk, maple syrup and butter to the bowl, but do not stir.
3. Heat in microwave on HIGH (100%) for 3 minutes.
4. Stir the walnuts into the fudge mixture until the fudge begins to thicken; pour into the lined baking dish. Smooth the top of the fudge with a spatula.
5. Refrigerate until firm, about 15 minutes. Remove the fudge from the pan using the cling film. Cut into small squares and store in an airtight container.

TIM TAM AND MILO FUDGE

Ingredients
395 g sweetened condensed milk
375 g milk chocolate melts
200 g Tim Tams, roughly chopped
65 g (½ cup) Milo or any malted milk powder

Method
1. Grease and line a 20 cm x 20 cm square baking tin with greasesafe baking paper and set aside.
2. Place the sweetened condensed milk and chocolate melts into a microwave-safe bowl.
3. Heat on MEDIUM (50%) in 30 second bursts, stirring each time with a dry metal spoon until just melted (this will take approximately 1-2 minutes).
4. Working quickly, stir through the chopped Tim Tams and Milo.
5. Pour into the prepared tin and place into the fridge for 2-3 hours to set.
6. Cut into small slices and serve.

RUSSIAN FUDGE

Ingredients
3 cups white sugar
200 ml (½ tin) condensed milk
125 g butter (125gms)
1 teaspoon vanilla essence
½ cup milk
1 tablespoon golden syrup
Pinch of salt
1 cup of chopped nuts (optional)

Method
1. Place all ingredients except nuts in a very large microwave-safe bowl.
2. Stir to mix and cook on high for 15-17 minutes, stirring well every 3 minutes.
3. Remove from microwave and beat until thick (approximately 5 minutes). Add nuts (if using) and pour into a greased tin, cut when set.

CHOCOLATE FUDGE

Ingredients
395 g sweetened condensed milk
50 g unsalted butter, cubed
350 g milk chocolate, roughly chopped

Method
1. Line a slice pan with baking paper and set aside.
2. In a microwave-safe bowl, place the butter and condensed milk and heat on high for 2 minutes.
3. Remove from microwave and add the milk chocolate. Stir constantly until chocolate is melted.
4. Pour mixture into the slice pan. Refrigerate until set which is approximately 2-4 hours. Slice into bite-sized pieces.

MACADAMIA FUDGE

Ingredients
400 g sweetened condensed milk
200 g white chocolate melts
125 g butter, chopped
1 cup brown sugar
2 tablespoons golden syrup
1 cup macadamias, roughly chopped
1 teaspoon vanilla essence

Method
1. Place condensed milk, chocolate, butter, sugar, and golden syrup in large microwave-safe bowl. Melt on HIGH (100%) for 5-7 minutes, stirring every 2 minutes.
2. Stir through nuts and vanilla. Pour into a paper-lined 18 cm x 28 cm baking tray.
3. Refrigerate for 4 hours or overnight until firm. Cut fudge into squares before serving.
4. Store in airtight container in refrigerator.

SALTED CARAMEL FUDGE

Ingredients
50 g unsalted butter
395 g sweetened condensed milk
500 g soft brown sugar
Good pinch sea salt (plus extra for sprinkling)
250 g white chocolate

Method
1. Grease and line an 18 x 28 cm rectangular slice tin with baking paper and set aside.
2. Place the butter, condensed milk and brown sugar into a microwave-safe bowl. Melt together in the microwave for 8 minutes (take out and stir every 2 minutes).
3. Stir through the sea salt and white chocolate melts.
4. Pour the fudge into the prepared tin and sprinkle over the extra sea salt.
5. Place into the fridge to set for 2 hours before cutting into pieces.

ROCKY ROAD FUDGE

Ingredients
395 g condensed milk
30 g butter
1 tablespoon golden syrup
375 g dark chocolate broken into pieces
200 g marshmallows chopped
1 cup peanuts crushed

Method
1. Line base and sides of a lamington tin with baking paper. In a microwave-safe bowl add condensed milk, butter and golden syrup.
2. Cook, uncovered, for 3-4 minutes on high until golden, stirring every minute.
3. Add chocolate and stir until melted. Stir marshmallows and nuts in quickly, mixing until combined.
4. Spread into prepared tin, refrigerate until set. Cut into squares to serve.

NOTES

www.ingramcontent.com/pod-product-compliance
Lightning Source LLC
Chambersburg PA
CBHW071941020426
42331CB00010B/2972